Johnny Cash

The Remarkable Journey Of The Man In Black

Jason Albright

Johnny cash

Copyright Page © **2023** by **Jason Albright**

All rights reserved. No part of this publication may be reproduced, distributed, or transmitted in any form or by any means, including photocopying, recording, or other electronic or mechanical methods, without the prior written permission of the publisher, except in the case of brief quotations embodied in critical reviews and certain other non-commercial uses permitted by copyright law.

Johnny cash

"I wear the black for those who've never read or listened to the words that Jesus said about the road to happiness through love and charity."

— Johnny Cash

Contents

Introduction 5

Early Life and Family 9

Career Adventures and Record Signings 15

Person life and legacy 37

Honors and Award 55

Other Media Explorations 59

Johnny cash

Introduction

John R. Cash, originally known as J. R. Cash, graced the American music scene with his deep, bass-baritone voice, leaving an indelible mark on the country genre. Born on February 26, 1932, in the humble town of Kingsland, Arkansas, his journey from impoverished cotton fields to international stardom is a testament to the enduring spirit of the American dream.

Cash's music, with its themes of sorrow, moral struggles, and redemption, evolved over the years. His signature Tennessee Three backing band provided a distinctive train-like chugging guitar rhythm that became a hallmark of his sound. What set Cash apart was not just his music but also his persona—a fusion of rebelliousness and an increasingly somber and humble demeanor.

After serving four years in the Air Force, Johnny Cash burst onto the music scene in the mid-1950s, making his mark in

Johnny cash

Memphis, Tennessee, within the burgeoning rockabilly scene. His concerts typically began with a simple introduction, "Hello, I'm Johnny Cash," a phrase that became synonymous with his name. "Folsom Prison Blues," one of his signature songs, often followed, setting the tone for a performance that would resonate with audiences for generations.

Among his repertoire of iconic songs, "I Walk the Line," "Ring of Fire," "Get Rhythm," and "Man in Black" stand out as testaments to his lyrical and musical prowess. Cash's range extended beyond the serious and introspective; he also recorded humorous tunes like "One Piece at a Time" and "A Boy Named Sue." His duets with his future wife June, including the classic "Jackson," became beloved hits. Johnny Cash's catalog also featured a collection of railroad songs, such as "Hey, Porter," "Orange Blossom Special," and "Rock Island Line."

In the latter phase of his illustrious career, Cash showcased his versatility by covering songs by contemporary rock artists.

Johnny cash

Notable among these covers were "Hurt" by Nine Inch Nails, "Rusty Cage" by Soundgarden, and "Personal Jesus" by Depeche Mode, displaying his ability to bridge the gap between generations and genres.

Cash's impact on the music industry is undeniable, evident in his record-breaking sales, with over 90 million records sold worldwide. His genre-spanning music encompassed country, rock and roll, rockabilly, blues, folk, and gospel, earning him a place in the hallowed halls of the Country Music, Rock and Roll, and Gospel Music Halls of Fame—a testament to his crossover appeal and enduring influence.

The life and career of Johnny Cash were vividly portrayed in the 2005 biopic "Walk the Line," where American film actor Joaquin Phoenix brought the iconic artist to life on the big screen.

Johnny cash

In this biography, we invite you to journey alongside Johnny Cash through the highs and lows of his remarkable life—a life that continues to resonate with music lovers and those who appreciate the authenticity and depth of an American legend.

Chapter 1

Early Life and Family

Johnny Cash's journey began in Kingsland, Arkansas, on February 26, 1932, as J. R. Cash, born to Carrie Cloveree (née Rivers) and Ray Cash. He came from a family of eight siblings, with three older siblings - Roy, Margaret Louise, and Jack - and three younger ones - Reba, Joanne, and Tommy, who would later become a renowned country artist in his own right. Cash's heritage was primarily English and Scottish, with a touch of Cherokee ancestry claimed by his paternal grandmother, though a DNA test of his daughter Rosanne found no Native American markers. He traced his Scottish surname back to the 11th-century Fife, and some places in Fife bear the name of his family. Interestingly, he was a distant cousin of British Conservative politician Sir William Cash.

Johnny cash

Johnny Cash's transformation from J. R. Cash into the iconic "Johnny Cash" began in 1955, when he signed with the legendary Sun Records. At this pivotal moment in his career, he decided to embrace a new stage name.

Prior to this, the naming process had been a compromise between his parents. His mother favored "John," while his father leaned towards "Ray." To reconcile their differences, they settled on the initials J. R. However, when he enlisted in the Air Force in 1950, regulations prohibited the use of initials as a first name. Consequently, he adjusted his name to "John R. Cash."

But it was his association with Sun Records that truly marked the birth of the Johnny Cash persona, a name that would become synonymous with country music legendry.

The Cash family's early years were marked by their move to Dyess, Arkansas, in March 1935. Dyess was a New Deal colony

Johnny cash

designed to provide opportunities for impoverished families to work the land and eventually become landowners. From the age of five, young Johnny toiled in the cotton fields alongside his family, their voices harmonizing as they worked. The Cash farm faced its share of hardships during the Great Depression, including a devastating flood that inspired Johnny to pen the song "Five Feet High and Rising." These struggles left an enduring mark on Cash, instilling in him a profound empathy for the struggles of the poor and working class, which would go on to influence many of his songs.

Tragedy struck in 1944 when Johnny's older brother Jack, with whom he shared a close bond, suffered a gruesome accident at work, nearly severed in two by an unguarded table saw. Despite a sense of foreboding that hung over that fateful day, with his mother urging Jack to skip work and go fishing, the family's financial needs led Jack to continue working. The guilt Johnny felt over his brother's death would stay with him throughout his life, and he often spoke of his anticipation of reuniting with Jack in the afterlife.

Johnny cash

From an early age, Cash's world was steeped in gospel music and the rhythms of the radio. His mother and a childhood friend taught him to play the guitar, igniting his passion for music and songwriting at just 12 years old. He sang on a local radio station during his high school years, and later in life, he released the album "My Mother's Hymn Book," a tribute to the gospel songs that shaped his youth. Additionally, traditional Irish music, which he regularly heard on the Jack Benny radio program, had a significant impact on his musical sensibilities.

Cash's journey took a different turn in 1950 when he enlisted in the Air Force. After finishing his initial training at Lackland Air Force Base in San Antonio, Texas, and his technical training at Brooks Air Force Base in the same city, he was sent to Landsberg, West Germany, to serve with the 12th Radio Squadron Mobile of the United States Air Force Security Service. There, he operated Morse code equipment, intercepting Soviet Army transmissions. It was during this

Johnny cash

service that Cash received the alleged news of Joseph Stalin's death via Morse code, a story corroborated by his daughter Rosanne. While stationed in Landsberg, he formed his first band, "The Landsberg Barbarians." On July 3, 1954, he was honorably discharged as a staff sergeant, and he returned to Texas, forever bearing a distinctive scar on the right side of his jaw, a reminder of a cyst removal surgery during his military service.

Johnny cash

Chapter 2

Career Adventures and Record Signings

In 1954, Johnny Cash, accompanied by his first wife, Vivian, made their way to Memphis, Tennessee, a city teeming with musical aspirations. Cash, who had previously worked selling appliances while honing his skills as a radio announcer, spent his evenings performing alongside guitarist Luther Perkins and bassist Marshall Grant. This dynamic trio, comprising Cash, Perkins, and Grant, became known as the Tennessee Two.

With dreams of securing a recording contract, Cash summoned the courage to visit the renowned Sun Records studio. There, he faced the legendary Sam Phillips, the label's producer. Cash's initial repertoire was predominantly gospel songs, only to discover that Phillips had moved on from

Johnny cash

recording gospel music. It's been rumored that Phillips told Cash to "go home and sin, then come back with a song I can sell." However, in a 2002 interview, Cash vehemently denied that Phillips made such a remark. Eventually, Cash managed to win over Phillips with a fresh set of songs, delivered in his early rockabilly style.

In 1955, Cash made his maiden recordings at Sun Records, which included tracks like "Hey Porter" and "Cry! Cry! Cry!". These songs became available for purchase towards the end of June in that year, swiftly gaining popularity on the country music charts.

A pivotal moment in music history occurred on December 4, 1956, when Elvis Presley made an unannounced visit to the Sun Records studio while Carl Perkins was recording new tracks with Jerry Lee Lewis on piano. Cash was also present in the studio, leading to an impromptu jam session that Phillips decided to capture on tape. The resulting recordings, encompassing both gospel and other songs, have been

Johnny cash

preserved and released as the "Million Dollar Quartet." Cash, as he later wrote in his autobiography, was positioned farthest from the microphone, adapting his voice to a higher pitch to blend in with Elvis.

Following this memorable moment, Cash continued to climb the charts with hits like "Folsom Prison Blues," which reached the country top five, and "I Walk the Line," a chart-topper in the country genre that also made its way into the pop charts' top 20. It was in July of 1957 that he made the recording for "Home of the Blues."

During the same year, Johnny Cash earned the distinction of being the first Sun Records artist to release a full-length album. Despite being the label's most consistent seller and prolific artist at the time, Cash felt constrained by his contract with Sun. Phillips was resistant to Cash recording gospel music and offered a 3% royalty rate instead of the standard 5%. Meanwhile, Phillips had shifted much of his attention and promotional efforts towards Jerry Lee Lewis.

Johnny cash

In 1958, Cash made a significant career move by signing a lucrative deal with Columbia Records. His single "Don't Take Your Guns to Town" emerged as one of his major hits during this period. He also recorded a collection of gospel songs for his second Columbia album. However, Cash left behind a substantial backlog of Sun Records recordings. Phillips kept putting out new singles and albums utilizing previously unreleased material all the way up until 1964. This unique situation saw Cash simultaneously releasing new music on two different labels.

Cash's distinctive choice of black clothing during his early career earned him the teasing nickname "the Undertaker" among fellow artists. His rationale was purely practical; black clothes were easier to keep looking clean during the rigors of extensive touring.

Johnny cash

In the early 1960s, Cash embarked on tours with the Carter Family, a group that now regularly included Mother Maybelle's daughters: Anita, June, and Helen. June Carter, in particular, would later recount her admiration for Cash from a distance during these tours. Cash also made appearances on Pete Seeger's brief television series, "Rainbow Quest." He ventured into acting, even composing and performing the opening theme for the 1961 film "Five Minutes to Live," later re-released as "Door-to-door Maniac."

During this phase, Cash's career was managed by Saul Holiff, a promoter from London, Ontario. The unique dynamics of their relationship would later serve as the subject of Saul Holiff's son's biopic, "My Father and the Man in Black."

Folsom and Other Prison Concerts

Johnny Cash's foray into prison concerts commenced in the late 1950s, with a landmark performance on January 1, 1958, at San Quentin State Prison. These prison concerts marked a

Johnny cash

pivotal phase in Cash's career, culminating in two highly acclaimed live albums: "Johnny Cash at Folsom Prison" (1968) and "Johnny Cash at San Quentin" (1969). These albums not only claimed the top spot on the Billboard country album chart but also witnessed "Johnny Cash at San Quentin" crossing over to dominate the Billboard pop album chart—a remarkable feat.

In 1969, Johnny Cash achieved an extraordinary milestone by outselling even The Beatles, with a staggering 6.5 million albums sold. This accomplishment underlined the extraordinary success of his jail concerts in comparison to his other live albums, These albums achieved relatively lower chart positions, with "Strawberry Cake" reaching number 33 and "Live at Madison Square Garden" securing the 39th spot on the charts.

"Johnny Cash at Folsom Prison" kicked off with a gripping rendition of his signature "Folsom Prison Blues," setting the tone for a momentous performance. Meanwhile, "Johnny Cash at San Quentin" featured the crossover sensation "A Boy

Johnny cash

Named Sue," a witty and catchy Shel Silverstein-penned novelty song that soared to the number one spot on the country charts and an impressive second place on the U.S. top-10 pop charts.

Cash's commitment to performing for incarcerated audiences extended internationally in 1972 when he took the stage at Sweden's Österåker Prison, resulting in the release of the live album "På Österåker" (At Österåker) in 1973. In this instance, Cash swapped "San Quentin" for "Österåker" in the song titles, showcasing his unwavering dedication to connecting with inmates worldwide.

In 1976, Cash's prison concert legacy continued with a concert at Tennessee State Prison, recorded for television broadcast. This memorable performance eventually received a belated CD release under the title "A Concert Behind Prison Walls" after Cash's passing, further cementing his impact on the prison concert genre.

Johnny cash

Native American advocacy

Johnny Cash leveraged his fame and financial resources to raise awareness about the issues affecting Native American communities. Through his music, Cash tackled topics surrounding indigenous humanity and confronted the U.S. government's treatment of Native Americans, a subject largely avoided by non-Native American artists.

In 1965, Cash and June Carter appeared on Pete Seeger's television show, "Rainbow Quest," where Cash discussed his early involvement as an activist for Native Americans. He expressed, In '57, I wrote a song called 'Old Apache Squaw,' and subsequently put aside the intended Indian protest theme for a while. However, it seemed like nobody else was addressing the issue with the same fervor."

Cash's record label at the time, Columbia Music, initially opposed including "Old Apache Squaw" on his upcoming album, deeming it "too radical for the public." His decision to

Johnny cash

sing about Indian tragedies and settler violence challenged the prevailing image of country music in the 1950s, which often romanticized cowboys as heroes who simply claimed native lands as their own.

Despite resistance, in 1964, Cash recorded the groundbreaking album "Bitter Tears: Ballads of the American Indian" after the success of his chart-topping album "I Walk the Line." This album featured stories of various Indigenous peoples, shedding light on their brutal oppression by white settlers. Cash, along with folk artist Peter La Farge, whom he greatly admired for his activism, co-wrote many of the protest songs on the album.

One of the album's standout tracks, "The Ballad of Ira Hayes," faced resistance from non-political radio stations and limited promotion from the record label due to its provocative and "unappealing" nature. Undeterred, Cash took matters into his own hands, posting an open letter in Billboard on August 22, 1964, challenging the industry's cowardice and urging radio stations to play the song. His perseverance paid off, with "The

Johnny cash

Ballad of Ira Hayes" eventually reaching number three on the country charts.

Cash continued to use "The Johnny Cash Show" as a platform to share stories of Native American struggles, both through song and short films, including the history of the Trail of Tears. In 1966, he was adopted by the Seneca Nation's Turtle Clan as a mark of recognition for his advocacy.

Cash's commitment extended to benefit concerts and fundraising efforts, such as supporting a school near the Rosebud Reservation, where a historical massacre had occurred. His unwavering activism for Native Americans left a lasting impact, demonstrating his dedication to using his influence and voice to address important social and humanitarian issues.

From June 1969 to March 1971, Johnny Cash took the television world by storm with "The Johnny Cash Show," a

Johnny cash

production that aired on the ABC network. Held at the historic Ryman Auditorium in Nashville, the show was a product of Screen Gems and featured some iconic acts. The Statler Brothers consistently opened each episode, setting the stage for a musical journey that included the legendary Carter Family and rockabilly icon Carl Perkins as regular fixtures.

But what made "The Johnny Cash Show" truly exceptional was its lineup of guest performers, including Linda Ronstadt in her television debut, musical giants like Neil Young, Louis Armstrong, Neil Diamond, Kenny Rogers and The First Edition (making four appearances), James Taylor, Ray Charles, Roger Miller, Roy Orbison, Derek and the Dominos, Joni Mitchell, and Bob Dylan.

In September 1969, Johnny Cash and Al Hurricane shared the stage during a series of four concerts at the New Mexico State Fair in Albuquerque, showcasing the power of their musical collaboration. During the same era, Cash contributed to the film "Little Fauss and Big Halsy," providing the title track,

Johnny cash

"The Ballad of Little Fauss and Big Halsy," penned by the illustrious Carl Perkins, which earned a Golden Globe award nomination in 1971.

Johnny Cash's friendship with Bob Dylan, cultivated in Woodstock, New York, was a remarkable musical alliance. They collaborated on the duet "Girl from the North Country," featured on Dylan's country album "Nashville Skyline." Cash even penned the Grammy-winning liner notes for this album.

A pivotal moment in the show was Kris Kristofferson's emergence as a singer-songwriter. Cash's refusal to change the lyrics of Kristofferson's "Sunday Mornin' Comin' Down," which referenced marijuana, during a live performance, showcased Cash's authenticity:

"On a Sunday morning sidewalk

I'm wishin', Lord, that I was stoned."

Johnny cash

"*The Johnny Cash Show*" concluded with a soul-stirring gospel music special, featuring luminaries such as the Blackwood Brothers, Mahalia Jackson, Stuart Hamblen, and Billy Graham.

Johnny Cash's iconic persona as the "Man in Black" was a defining aspect of his career. He donned all-black attire, including his signature long, black, knee-length coat, which was a stark contrast to the glitzy rhinestone suits and cowboy boots worn by many of his contemporaries. Cash explained that he wore black as a symbol of solidarity with the downtrodden—the poor, the incarcerated, and those who had paid for their mistakes. He also expressed his mourning for lives lost in the Vietnam War and a world still rife with poverty, neglect, and suffering.

While the initial reason for wearing black was practical, Cash embraced it as his on-stage persona. He pointed out that he liked the color black for its aesthetic appeal. Interestingly, the US Navy's winter blue uniform, featuring a black shirt, tie, and

Johnny cash

trousers, was humorously referred to by sailors as "Johnny Cashes" in homage to his iconic fashion sense.

In the early 1970s, Cash's chart-topping hits began to wane, and he ventured into commercial endorsements, including Amoco and STP, during the energy crisis of the 1970s. In 1976, he even lent his talents to commercials for Lionel Trains, composing the music for them.

Cash's unyielding friendship with Billy Graham led to his involvement in producing "Gospel Road: A Story of Jesus," a film in which he co-wrote and narrated. This project was a personal expression of faith for Cash rather than an instrument for proselytization.

Throughout his career, Cash continued to incorporate gospel and religious songs into his albums, and he made appearances on various television shows, including hosting Christmas specials on CBS. He also ventured into acting, with notable

Johnny cash

roles in "Columbo" and "Little House on the Prairie." His portrayal of abolitionist John Brown in the 1985 American Civil War miniseries "North and South" showcased his versatility.

Notably, Johnny Cash's friendships extended to several US presidents, including his performance at the White House in 1970 for President Richard Nixon. While Nixon's office had suggested specific songs, Cash chose to perform different ones due to logistical reasons, a decision that was not politically motivated.

Cash's enduring impact was further solidified when he became the grand marshal of the United States Bicentennial parade, donning a shirt designed by Nudie Cohn. After the parade, he delivered a memorable concert at the Washington Monument.

In 1980, Johnny Cash achieved the distinction of becoming the youngest living inductee into the Country Music Hall of

Johnny cash

Fame, a remarkable honor at the age of 48. However, as the 1980s progressed, his record releases struggled to make significant waves on the country music charts, even though his live performances continued to draw substantial audiences. During the mid-1980s, Cash embarked on a musical journey with three other iconic artists: Waylon Jennings, Willie Nelson, and Kris Kristofferson, collectively known as The Highwaymen. Their collaboration resulted in three hit albums: "Highwayman" in 1985, "Highwaymen 2" in 1990, and "Highwaymen – The Road Goes On Forever" in 1995.

Throughout this period, Cash ventured into television films, notably starring in "The Pride of Jesse Hallam" in 1981, a film that garnered praise for raising awareness about adult illiteracy. In 1983, he took on the role of a heroic sheriff in "Murder in Coweta County," a film based on a real-life murder case in Georgia, co-starring Andy Griffith as his antagonist.

In 1983, Cash faced a challenging setback when he suffered a severe abdominal injury caused by an unfortunate encounter

Johnny cash

with an ostrich on his farm. This incident led to a relapse into addiction after receiving painkillers.

In 1988, while visiting Waylon Jennings in the hospital as he recovered from a heart attack, Jennings advised Cash to seek medical attention for his own heart condition. Subsequently, doctors recommended preventive heart surgery, and Cash underwent double bypass surgery in the same hospital. Both artists recovered, with Cash making a notable decision to avoid prescription painkillers to prevent a return to dependency. He later described this period as a time when he had a "near-death experience" during his operation.

In 1984, Cash released a unique recording titled "The Chicken in Black," which humorously imagined his brain being transplanted into a chicken while receiving a bank robber's brain in return. Contrary to some claims that he recorded this intentionally poor song in protest of Columbia Records, biographer Robert Hilburn contended that it was Columbia that presented Cash with the song. Cash enthusiastically

Johnny cash

embraced it, even performing it live on stage and creating a comedic music video in which he donned a superhero-like bank-robber costume. However, his enthusiasm waned after Waylon Jennings commented that he looked like a "buffoon" in the video, leading Cash to demand that Columbia withdraw the music video from broadcast and recall the single from stores, interrupting its chart success and deeming the venture "a fiasco."

Between 1981 and 1984, Cash recorded several sessions with famed countrypolitan producer Billy Sherrill, which remained unreleased until 2014 when they were published by Columbia's sister label, Legacy Recordings, under the title "Out Among the Stars." Around the same period, Cash recorded a gospel album, which was ultimately released by another label due to Columbia closing its Priority Records division, originally slated to release the recordings.

Johnny cash

Following the release of several unsuccessful recordings between 1984 and 1985, Cash parted ways with Columbia Records.

In 1986, Cash made a return to Sun Studios in Memphis, where he collaborated with Roy Orbison, Jerry Lee Lewis, and Carl Perkins to produce the album "Class of '55." Remarkably, Cash was still under contract with Columbia Records at the time, necessitating special arrangements to enable his participation in this project. In the same year, he published his sole novel, "Man in White," a narrative exploring the conversion of Saul into the Apostle Paul. Furthermore, in 1990, Johnny Cash recorded an album titled "Johnny Cash Reads The Complete New Testament."

Subsequent to being dropped by Columbia Records, Cash signed a contract with Mercury Records from 1987 to 1991. During this period, he recorded a collection of new versions of his well-known Sun and Columbia hits. He also collaborated on the album "Water from the Wells of Home," featuring

Johnny cash

duets with his children Rosanne Cash and John Carter Cash, as well as Paul McCartney. Following his Mercury contract, he released a one-off Christmas album on the Delta Records label.

Though Cash did not produce any chart-topping hits between 1991 and his passing, he experienced a resurgence in his career during the 1990s, attracting a broader audience not traditionally associated with country music. In 1988, British post-punk musicians Marc Riley and Jon Langford organized "Til Things Are Brighter," a tribute album featuring interpretations of Cash's songs by British-based indie-rock acts. Cash embraced the project, finding it uplifting, and it received attention on both sides of the Atlantic. He continued to make unexpected musical contributions, including a version of "Man in Black" for the Christian punk band One Bad Pig's 1991 album "I Scream Sunday" and singing "The Wanderer," written by Bono, as the closing track on U2's 1993 album "Zooropa."

Johnny cash

Cash's fortunes were revitalized when he signed with Rick Rubin's American Recordings label. His first album under Rubin's guidance, "American Recordings," released in 1994, was a stripped-down, intimate affair, recorded in his living room with just his trusty Martin Dreadnought guitar. It featured covers of songs by contemporary artists handpicked by Rubin and earned a Grammy for Best Contemporary Folk Album. Cash treasured his performance at the 1994 Glastonbury Festival as one of the highlights of his career. This marked the beginning of a decade of critical acclaim and commercial success. He joined forces with Brooks & Dunn to contribute "Folsom Prison Blues" to the AIDS benefit album "Red Hot + Country" produced by the Red Hot Organization. On that very album, he rendered Bob Dylan's classic "Forever Young."

Also in the esteemed television series "Dr. Quinn, Medicine Woman," both Johnny Cash and his wife June Carter Cash made brief cameo appearances. In addition to this, Cash provided his voice for a one-of-a-kind cameo appearance in an

Johnny cash

episode of "The Simpsons" titled "El Viaje Misterioso de Nuestro Jomer (The Mysterious Voyage of Homer),". In that particular episode, Johnny played the role of the character known as the "Space Coyote," who acted as a shamanistic advisor to the character Homer Simpson. Johnny is credited with creating the character. Homer had a life-changing and unforgettable experience thanks to the guidance of this guide.

In 1996, Cash collaborated with Tom Petty and the Heartbreakers on "Unchained" (also known as American Recordings II), which won the Grammy for Best Country Album in 1998. This album, produced by Rick Rubin with Sylvia Massy engineering and mixing, included guest appearances by Lindsey Buckingham, Mick Fleetwood, and Marty Stuart. Believing that his 1975 autobiography, "Man in Black," didn't sufficiently explain his life, Cash authored "Cash: The Autobiography" in 1997.

Chapter 3

Person life and legacy

Johnny Cash's personal life and legacy are marked by a series of significant events and transformations. On July 18, 1951, while undergoing Air Force basic training, Cash encountered a 17-year-old Italian-American named Vivian Liberto at a roller skating rink in San Antonio, Texas. Their whirlwind romance lasted for three weeks until Cash was deployed to West Germany for a three-year tour. Despite the physical distance, their love story endured through hundreds of heartfelt love letters. Their enduring connection led to their marriage on August 7, 1954, at St. Ann's Roman Catholic Church in San Antonio. Collectively, the couple had four female offspring, namely Rosanne, Kathy, Cindy, and Tara. In 1961, Cash relocated his family to a hilltop home overlooking Casitas Springs, California. Prior to this, he had moved his parents to the area to manage a small trailer park known as the Johnny Cash Trailer Park. Unfortunately, Cash's struggle with alcohol and his numerous run-ins with local law enforcement strained

Johnny cash

his first marriage. Vivian Liberto later revealed that she filed for divorce in 1966 due to Cash's severe substance abuse, including drugs and alcohol, his extensive touring schedule, infidelity, and his close relationship with singer June Carter. As a result, their four daughters were primarily raised by their mother.

Johnny Cash's life took a pivotal turn when he crossed paths with June Carter of the renowned Carter Family while on tour. Their infatuation with each other grew over time, and in 1968, after a thirteen-year courtship that began backstage at the Grand Ole Opry, Cash proposed to June during a live performance in London, Ontario. They exchanged vows and became officially married on March 1, 1968, in Franklin, Kentucky. Together, they welcomed a son, John Carter Cash, born on March 3, 1970, making him the only son for both Johnny and June. Cash not only looked after his own children but also wholeheartedly embraced the role of stepfather to Carlene and Rosie. These two were June's daughters from her previous marriages to honky-tonk singer Carl Smith and

Johnny cash

Edwin "Rip" Nix, who was a former police officer, football player, and race-car driver. Johnny and June Carter Cash continued to work, create music, and tour together for an astonishing 35 years until June's passing in May 2003. Throughout their marriage, June played a pivotal role in trying to help Cash overcome his addiction, often confiscating and discarding his drugs. Even through multiple admissions for rehabilitation and decades of battling addiction, June stood by his side. After her passing, Johnny Cash found his solace in his music and passed away a mere four months later.

Amid the highs of his career in the late 1950s, Cash began to struggle with alcoholism and developed addictions to amphetamines and barbiturates. During this period, he shared an apartment in Nashville with Waylon Jennings, who was similarly entrenched in an amphetamine addiction. Cash used these stimulants to stay awake during demanding tours, and his "nervousness" and erratic behavior became the subject of jokes among friends. His version of "Ring of Fire" became a breakout hit, reaching number one on the country charts and entering the top 20 on the pop charts. This iconic song, originally performed by June's sister, featured Cash's distinctive mariachi-style horn arrangement, which he claimed came to him in a dream. Vivian Liberto later presented a different account of the song's origins, asserting that Cash awarded Carter half of the songwriting credit for financial reasons.

In June 1965, Cash's life took a dangerous turn when his camper caught fire during a fishing trip with his nephew Damon Fielder in Los Padres National Forest, California. This incident triggered a forest fire that nearly claimed his life. Cash attributed the fire to sparks from a faulty exhaust system in his camper, while Fielder believed that Cash, in a drugged state, unintentionally allowed the fire to escalate out of control while attempting to stay warm. In response to a lawsuit filed by the federal government, Cash settled and paid $82,001 for the damages caused by the fire, which destroyed 508 acres, consumed the foliage on three mountains, and drove off 49 of the refuge's 53 endangered California condors. Cash displayed

Johnny cash

little remorse, famously stating, "I don't care about your damn yellow buzzards."

Despite multiple run-ins with the law, Cash remarkably never served a prison sentence. Although he was briefly incarcerated seven times for misdemeanors, each stay lasted only a single night. Notably, he was arrested in Starkville, Mississippi, on May 11, 1965, for trespassing onto private property late at night to pick flowers. In another incident in El Paso, Texas, on October 4, 1965, Cash was arrested by a narcotics squad, suspected of smuggling heroin from Mexico. However, the authorities discovered prescription drugs – 688 Dexedrine capsules (amphetamines) and 475 Equanil tablets (sedatives) – hidden in his guitar case instead of illegal narcotics. As these pills were prescription drugs, Cash received a suspended sentence, posted a $1,500 bond, and was released until his arraignment.

During the mid-1960s, Cash embarked on

Johnny cash

a period of releasing concept albums. "Bitter Tears," released in 1964, was a notable album devoted to spoken word and songs addressing the plight of Native Americans and government mistreatment. Although it initially reached the charts, the album faced resistance from some fans and radio stations due to its controversial stance on social issues. In 2011, a book was published about this album, leading to a re-recording of its songs by contemporary artists and the production of a documentary film chronicling Cash's efforts. His "Sings the Ballads of the True West" album, released in 1965, was an innovative double record that combined authentic frontier songs with Cash's spoken narration.

Johnny Cash's life took a dramatic turn as he grappled with severe drug addiction and destructive behavior, leading to the end of his first marriage. However, during this period, he continued to achieve musical success, and in 1967, his duet with June Carter, "Jackson," won a Grammy Award.

Johnny cash

Cash's last arrest occurred in 1967 in Walker County, Georgia, after being found with a bag of prescription pills following a car accident. While in jail, Sheriff Ralph Jones delivered a heartfelt talk to Cash, emphasizing the dangers of his behavior and untapped potential. This encounter played a pivotal role in Cash's journey toward recovery, prompting him to change his life around. He returned to LaFayette, Georgia, to perform a benefit concert that drew an astounding 12,000 attendees, raising $75,000 for the local high school. In a 1997 interview, Cash reflected on his past struggles, acknowledging, "I was taking the pills for a while, and then the pills started taking me." June, along with other family members, including Maybelle and Ezra Carter, moved into Cash's mansion for a month to help him overcome his addiction. Johnny Cash proposed to June on stage during a concert in February 1968, and they married a week later, as he had successfully cleaned up his life.

Johnny Cash's transformation also included a renewed commitment to his Christian faith. He underwent a spiritual

Johnny cash

awakening and took an "altar call" at Evangel Temple, a small church in the Nashville area led by Reverend Jimmie Rodgers Snow, the son of country music legend Hank Snow. Cash's journey involved periods of drug use, relapse, and rehabilitation. In 1970, after the birth of his son, John Carter Cash, he fully embraced sobriety, staying drug-free for seven years. He struggled with substance abuse once again in 1977 and sought treatment at the Betty Ford Clinic in Rancho Mirage in 1983. By 1989, his dependence on drugs had resurfaced, leading him to the Cumberland Heights Alcohol and Drug Treatment Center in Nashville. In 1992, he entered the Loma Linda Behavioral Medicine Center in California for his final rehabilitation treatment. His son also sought treatment there several months later.

Cash's deep-rooted religious beliefs played a pivotal role in his life. He was raised in the Southern Baptist denomination of Christianity and was baptized in 1944 in the Tyronza River as a member of the Central Baptist Church of Dyess, Arkansas. Troubled but devout, Cash's spiritual journey was

Johnny cash

characterized by complexity and contradictions. He wrote a Christian novel titled "Man in White" in 1986, emphasizing his commitment to Christianity without confining himself to a specific denomination. In a 1997 interview, Cash firmly stated, "I'm a Christian. Don't put me in another box."

In the mid-1970s, Johnny and June Carter Cash pursued a course of study in the Bible through Christian International Bible College, which culminated in a pilgrimage to Israel in November 1978. During this period, Cash was ordained as a minister and officiated at his daughter's wedding. He frequently performed at Billy Graham Crusades and used his music to spread his faith. In 1986, at a Tallahassee Crusade, Johnny and June sang "One of These Days I'm Gonna Sit Down and Talk to Paul," and in 1989, he delivered a powerful message about salvation for drug dealers and alcoholics during a performance in Arkansas. Johnny Cash's spiritual journey and dedication to sharing his faith made a profound impact on those around him.

Johnny cash

Johnny Cash's legacy is one that encompasses both his enduring musical contributions and his personal battles and transformations. He is celebrated not only for his iconic music but also for his complex and multifaceted life journey.

Later years

In his later years, Johnny Cash faced significant health challenges. During a trip to New York City in 1997, he received a diagnosis of Shy–Drager syndrome, a neurodegenerative disease related to multiple system atrophy. Initially, his condition was mistakenly diagnosed as Parkinson's disease. In fact, Cash even informed his audience during a concert in Flint, Michigan, on October 25, 1997, that he had Parkinson's disease after nearly collapsing on stage. Subsequently, his diagnosis was corrected to Shy–Drager syndrome, and he was given approximately 18 months to live. Later, the diagnosis was again adjusted, this time to autonomic neuropathy linked to diabetes. This debilitating illness forced Cash to scale back his touring. In 1998, he was hospitalized due to severe pneumonia, which caused damage to his lungs.

Johnny cash

During the twilight of his career, Johnny Cash released two notable albums: "American III: Solitary Man" in 2000 and "American IV: The Man Comes Around" in 2002. "American IV" featured covers of songs by late 20th-century rock artists, including "Hurt" by Nine Inch Nails and "Personal Jesus" by Depeche Mode. Trent Reznor, the frontman of Nine Inch Nails, initially had reservations about Cash covering "Hurt" but was later deeply impressed by Cash's rendition. The music video for "Hurt" received both critical acclaim and widespread popularity, including a Grammy Award.

Tragedy struck in Johnny Cash's life when his beloved wife, June Carter Cash, passed away on May 15, 2003, at the age of 73. However, June had encouraged Cash to continue working, so he persevered and recorded an astounding 60 songs in the last four months of his life. He even surprised audiences with impromptu performances at the Carter Family Fold near Bristol, Virginia. At his last public performance on July 5,

Johnny cash

2003, before singing "Ring of Fire," Cash delivered a heartfelt statement:

"The spirit of June Carter overshadows me tonight with the love she had for me and the love I have for her. We connect somewhere between here and Heaven. She came down for a short visit, I guess, from Heaven to visit with me tonight to give me courage and inspiration like she always has. She's never been one for me except courage and inspiration. I thank God for June Carter. I love her with all my heart."

Cash's dedication to his music endured, and he continued to record until shortly before his passing. He once stated, "When June died, it tore him up," according to producer Rick Rubin. "He said to me, 'You have to keep me working because I will die if I don't have something to do.'" Despite being confined to a wheelchair, Cash recorded his final tracks on August 21, 2003. These included "Like the 309," which appeared on the 2006 album "American V: A Hundred Highways," and

Johnny cash

"Engine 143," recorded for his son John Carter Cash's planned Carter Family tribute album.

Johnny Cash's health deteriorated, and he was hospitalized at Baptist Hospital in Nashville. Tragically, he passed away at around 2:00 am Central Time on September 12, 2003, at the age of 71, less than four months after his beloved wife June's death. His final resting place is alongside hers at Hendersonville Memory Gardens near his home in Hendersonville, Tennessee.

Johnny Cash's legacy extends far beyond his music. He was not only a music icon but also a champion for artists on the fringes of country music, often defending those who pushed the boundaries of the genre, like Bob Dylan. In 1999, an all-star concert paid tribute to Cash, featuring a diverse group of artists such as Dylan, Chris Isaak, Wyclef Jean, Norah Jones, Kris Kristofferson, Willie Nelson, Dom DeLuise, and U2. Cash himself performed at the end of the event. Two tribute albums, "Kindred Spirits" featuring established artists and

Johnny cash

"Dressed in Black" featuring lesser-known musicians, were released shortly before his passing.

In his lifetime, Johnny Cash wrote over 1,000 songs and released numerous albums. A posthumous box set titled "Unearthed" was issued, featuring four CDs of previously unreleased material recorded with Rick Rubin, as well as a retrospective CD titled "Best of Cash on American." The box set also included a 104-page book that delved into each track and featured one of Cash's final interviews.

Cash's contributions to music were celebrated with numerous accolades. He was honored with a Lifetime Achievement Grammy in 1999. In the world of musical acclaim, Johnny Cash found himself sitting at a prestigious table. In 2004, Rolling Stone magazine bestowed upon him the 31st spot in their "100 Greatest Artists of All Time" list, a tribute to his enduring legacy. Then, in 2010, Cash's resonant voice and soulful expressions earned him an impressive 21st place on Rolling Stone's "100 Greatest Singers" list, solidifying his status

Johnny cash

as an icon for the ages. In 2012, Rolling Stone recognized Cash's albums "At Folsom Prison" and "American Recordings" on its list of the 500 greatest albums of all time.

In addition to his musical legacy, Johnny Cash was known for his philanthropy, particularly his support for SOS Children's Villages. The Johnny Cash Memorial Fund was established in his memory to continue this support.

In 2006, a limited-edition Forever stamp featuring Johnny Cash was released. It showcased a promotional image of Cash from around the 1963 release of "Ring of Fire: The Best of Johnny Cash."

Several tributes and honors have been bestowed on Johnny Cash posthumously, including the naming of "Johnny Cash Parkway" in Hendersonville, Tennessee, and the opening of the Johnny Cash Museum in Nashville. Additionally, in 2014, the Johnny Cash Trail, a multi-use bike trail with public art

Johnny cash

pieces celebrating Cash's life, was unveiled in Starkville, Mississippi. In 2015,

a new species of black tarantula was named Aphonopelma johnnycashi in his honor.

Cash's enduring impact is reflected in his portrayals in the media. The biographical film "Walk the Line" was released in 2005, featuring Joaquin Phoenix as Johnny Cash and Reese Witherspoon as June Carter Cash. The film garnered critical acclaim and commercial success, with Phoenix and Witherspoon receiving Academy Awards for their roles. In addition to the film, Johnny Cash's life has been portrayed in various stage productions, including "Ring of Fire" and "Million Dollar Quartet."

Robert Hilburn, a veteran Los Angeles Times pop music critic who had extensive interviews with Cash and accompanied him during his 1968 Folsom prison tour, published a comprehensive biography in 2013. This biography, spanning

Johnny cash

688 pages and featuring 16 pages of photographs, provided detailed insights into Cash's life, shedding light on the 80% of his life previously unknown, including his battles with addiction and infidelity.

Johnny cash

Chapter 4

Honors and Award

Johnny Cash's remarkable career garnered a multitude of awards and accolades spanning nearly five decades. He was a true icon of country music and transcended genres, leaving a lasting impact on various musical styles, including rock and roll, blues, rockabilly, folk, and gospel.

His extensive list of awards includes multiple Country Music Association (CMA) Awards, Grammy Awards, and recognition in categories such as vocal and spoken performances, album notes, and videos. Johnny Cash was celebrated as the embodiment of country music for countless fans worldwide.

What truly set Cash apart was his versatility as a musician. He effortlessly ventured into different musical realms, producing songs that defied a single genre classification. His influence reached far and wide, touching the realms of rock and roll, blues, rockabilly, folk, and gospel.

Johnny cash

Johnny Cash's remarkable contributions to music earned him well-deserved recognition in five major music halls of fame. These honors consisted of his induction into the Memphis Music Hall of Fame in 2013, followed by his inclusion in the GMA's Gospel Music Hall of Fame in 2010. In 1992, he became a member of the Rock and Roll Hall of Fame, and a decade earlier in 1980, he was honored with a place in the Country Music Hall of Fame. His journey through these halls of fame began in 1977 when he was inducted into the Nashville Songwriters Hall of Fame.

One remarkable fact that attested to his legendary status was his dual induction into the Country Music Hall of Fame and the Rock and Roll Hall of Fame. Rolling Stone, recognizing his significance, noted that apart from Elvis Presley, Cash was the only artist to achieve this distinction as a performer.

Cash's impact on the music world earned him a place in the Rockabilly Hall of Fame. Furthermore, his outstanding contributions to the arts were commemorated with the prestigious Kennedy Center Honors in 1996. For Johnny Cash, his induction into the Country Music Hall of Fame in 1980 stood as the pinnacle of his professional achievements.

Johnny cash

In 2001, he received the esteemed National Medal of Arts, further solidifying his position as a cultural and musical icon. The music video for "Hurt" brought him into the MTV generation, earning six nominations at the 2003 MTV Video Music Awards. While it secured the award for Best Cinematography, it also marked Johnny Cash as the oldest artist ever nominated for an MTV Video Music Award.

The impact of Johnny Cash's music was so profound that even contemporary artists recognized his influence. Justin Timberlake, upon winning a VMA in 2003, acknowledged Cash's legacy and expressed that he believed Cash deserved the recognition more than anyone.

Johnny Cash's remarkable journey through the world of music left an indelible mark, and his recognition and honors stand as a testament to his enduring legacy.

Johnny cash

Chapter 5

Other Media Explorations

FILMOGRAPHY

Johnny Cash had a notable career in film and television in addition to his music career. Here's a list of some of his most significant film and television appearances and the roles he played:

1. *Five Minutes to Live (1961)* - Role: Johnny Cabot

   - A crime drama film where Johnny Cash played the character of Johnny Cabot, a bank robber.

2. *The Hunted (2003)* - Role: The Narrator

3. *The Road to Nashville (1967)* - Role: Himself

Johnny cash

- A musical drama film where Johnny Cash appeared as himself.

4. *A Gunfight (1971)* - Role: Abe Cross

- A Western film in which Cash played the role of Abe Cross, a gunfighter.

5. *The Gospel Road: A Story of Jesus (1973)* - Role: Narrator

- Cash narrated this film, which tells the story of Jesus Christ.

6. *Stagecoach (1986)* - Role: Marshal Curly Wilcox

- A made-for-TV movie where Cash played the role of Marshal Curly Wilcox, a character from the classic Western story.

Television Appearances:

Johnny cash

1. *The Johnny Cash Show (1969-1971)* - Role: Host

   - Cash hosted his own musical variety show, featuring various guest artists.

2. *Little House on the Prairie (1976)* - Role: Caleb Hodgekiss

   - Cash guest-starred in this popular series as Caleb Hodgekiss, a charismatic con man.

3. *Columbo: Swan Song (1974)* - Role: Tommy Brown

   - Cash appeared in the detective series as Tommy Brown, a country music star.

4. *Murder in Coweta County (1983)* - Role: Lamar Potts

   - A TV movie where Cash portrayed Lamar Potts, a wealthy landowner involved in a murder case.

Johnny cash

5. *The Last Days of Frank and Jesse James (1986)* - Role: Frank James

   - Cash played the role of Frank James, the famous outlaw, in this TV movie.

6. *North and South (1986)* - Role: John Brown

   - Cash had a role as John Brown in the mini-series "North and South."

7. *The Hunt for Red October (1990)* - Role: Captain Mancuso

   - Cash made a brief appearance as Captain Mancuso in this film adaptation of Tom Clancy's novel.

8. *Dr. Quinn, Medicine Woman (1993-1994)* - Role: Kid Cole

   - Cash had a recurring role as Kid Cole, a former gunslinger turned preacher, in this TV series.

Johnny cash

Can I Ask For A Favour?

If you appreciated this book or found it helpful in any way, I would really appreciate it if you would take a few minutes to write a brief review on Amazon. I read each and every review and incorporate the feedback into my future projects.

A heartfelt "**Thank You**" for your help.

Printed in Great Britain
by Amazon